GORGAN
جرجان

همدان

HAMADAN

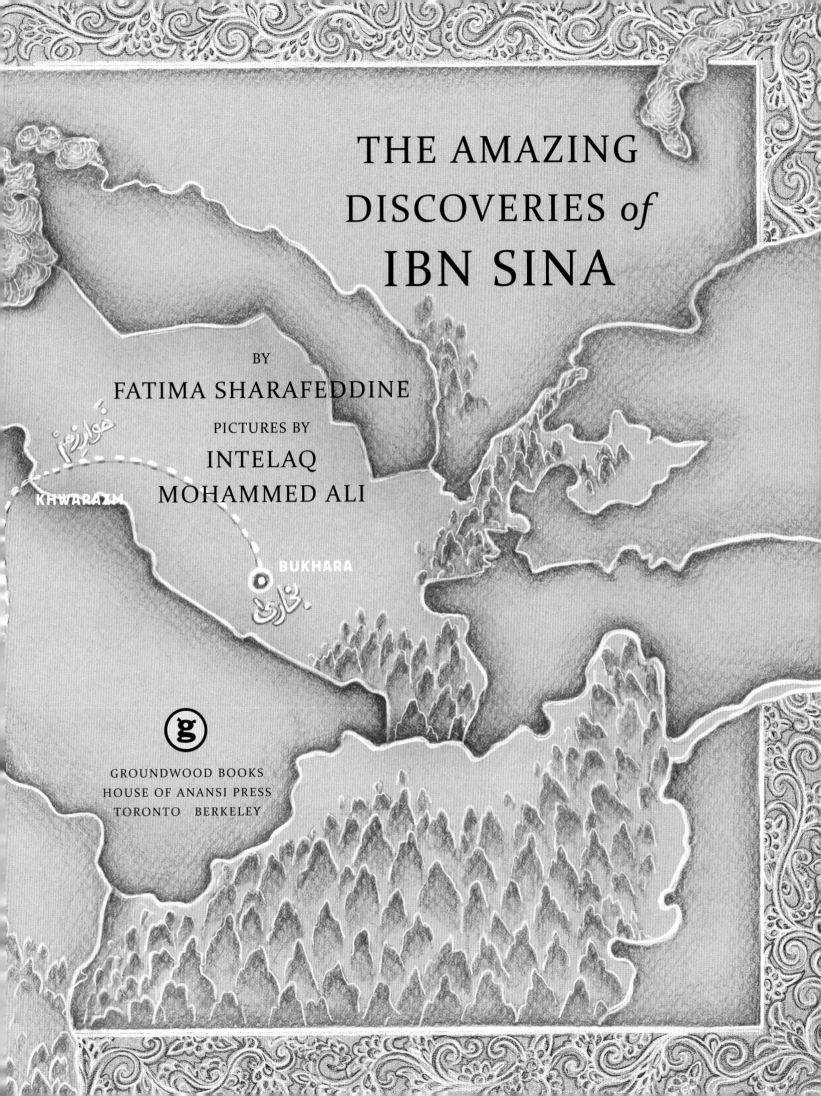

THE AMAZING DISCOVERIES of IBN SINA

BY

FATIMA SHARAFEDDINE

PICTURES BY

INTELAQ MOHAMMED ALI

KHWARAZM خوارزم

BUKHARA بخاری

GROUNDWOOD BOOKS
HOUSE OF ANANSI PRESS
TORONTO   BERKELEY

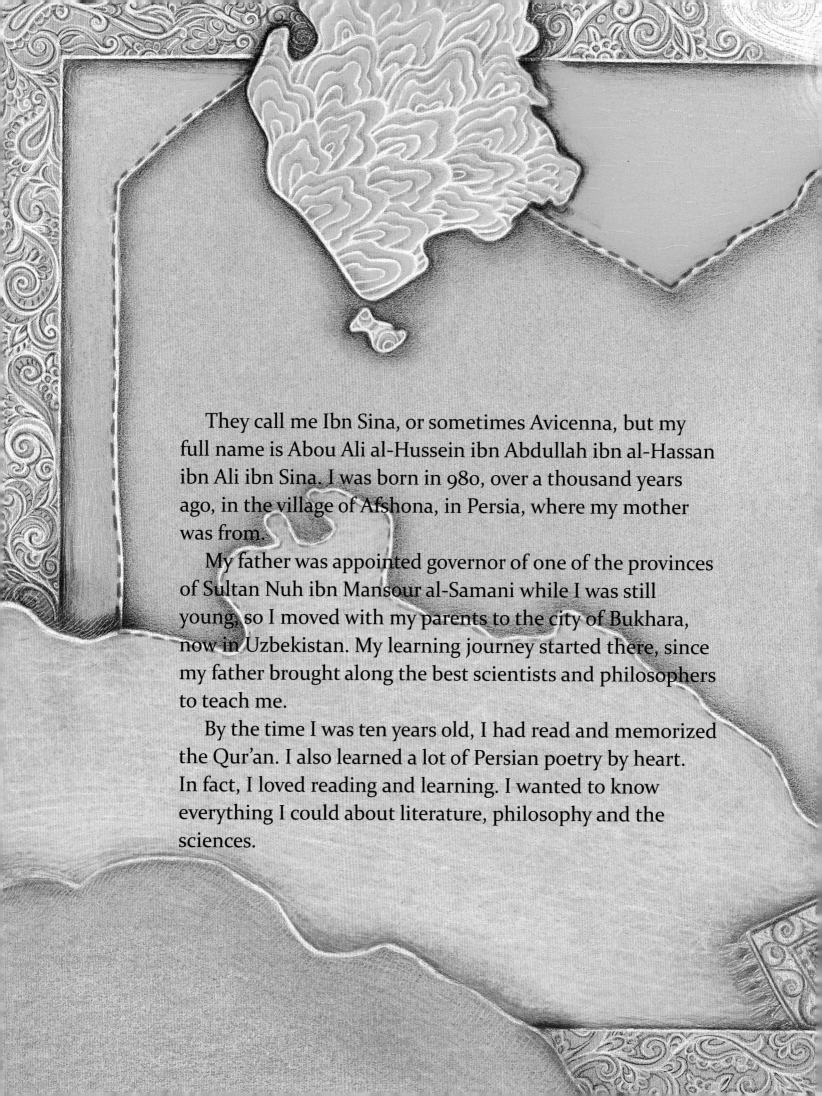

They call me Ibn Sina, or sometimes Avicenna, but my full name is Abou Ali al-Hussein ibn Abdullah ibn al-Hassan ibn Ali ibn Sina. I was born in 980, over a thousand years ago, in the village of Afshona, in Persia, where my mother was from.

My father was appointed governor of one of the provinces of Sultan Nuh ibn Mansour al-Samani while I was still young, so I moved with my parents to the city of Bukhara, now in Uzbekistan. My learning journey started there, since my father brought along the best scientists and philosophers to teach me.

By the time I was ten years old, I had read and memorized the Qur'an. I also learned a lot of Persian poetry by heart. In fact, I loved reading and learning. I wanted to know everything I could about literature, philosophy and the sciences.

بخاری

BUKHARA

My biggest passion was for studying medicine, and I used to pore over the books recommended by my professors. I completed my medical studies at the age of sixteen. During this time I discovered new ways of treating diseases that doctors had been unable to cure.

My relatives and friends were amazed by the speed with which I mastered the field of medicine. But I remember telling them that medicine was not a hard science to learn, so it was not surprising to excel in a short time.

In philosophy and logic, I was tutored by Abdullah al-Naeli, whose nickname was the Philosopher. He happened to be visiting Bukhara, so my father invited him to stay with us and asked him to tutor me.

But in my opinion, the Philosopher did not have a deep understanding of these subjects, so I started reading books about philosophy and logic on my own. I do not deny that I found these subjects complex, and it took quite some time to master them. What was most difficult was the book *Metaphysics* by the Greek philosopher Aristotle. I had to read it four times to fully grasp its contents.

In the evening, when it grew dark, I would light my lamp and continue reading and taking notes. If I felt tired or sleepy, I would have something to drink to restore my energy, then go back to my books.

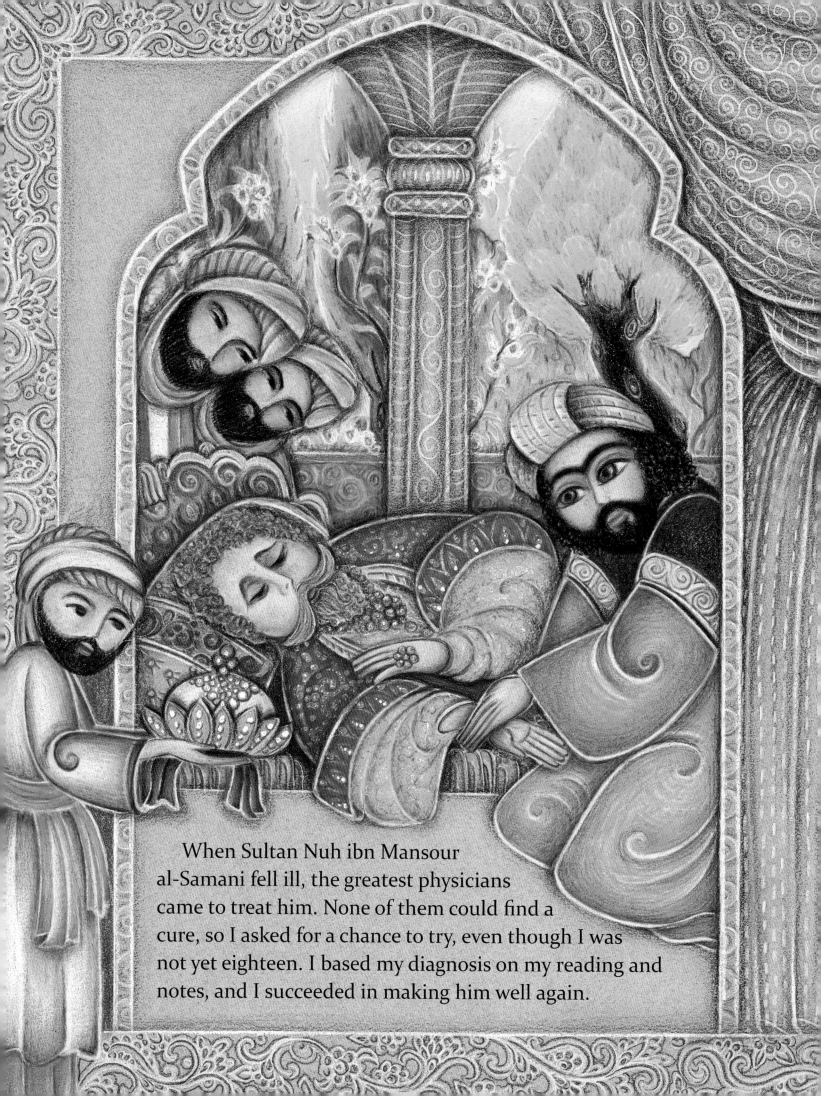

When Sultan Nuh ibn Mansour al-Samani fell ill, the greatest physicians came to treat him. None of them could find a cure, so I asked for a chance to try, even though I was not yet eighteen. I based my diagnosis on my reading and notes, and I succeeded in making him well again.

When the sultan was completely healed, he expressed his extreme appreciation by offering me a golden opportunity. He invited me to stay at his palace and have total access to his personal library. That was how I had the chance to read a great number of books on Islamic law, literature, philosophy, medicine, music, meteorology and architecture.

I was a very studious person who accepted challenges and explored subjects deeply. For example, after a discussion with a prominent linguist, I discovered that my knowledge of linguistics was incomplete. And so I immersed myself in the subject for three years until I reached a level of great understanding. Afterwards I wrote three poems in which I included vocabulary that would be unfamiliar to most readers.

I stayed in Bukhara until I was twenty-two years old, when my
father passed away and the rule of Sultan Nuh ibn Mansour al-Samani
ended. After that I moved a lot, living in different cities in Persia for
many years at a time. In Gorgan, near the Caspian Sea, I met a friend
who opened a school where I taught logic and astronomy. I spent time
in Ray, then Hamadan, where I became the medical attendant of the
ruler, al-Buwayhid, and was promoted to the office of vizier.

HAMADAN

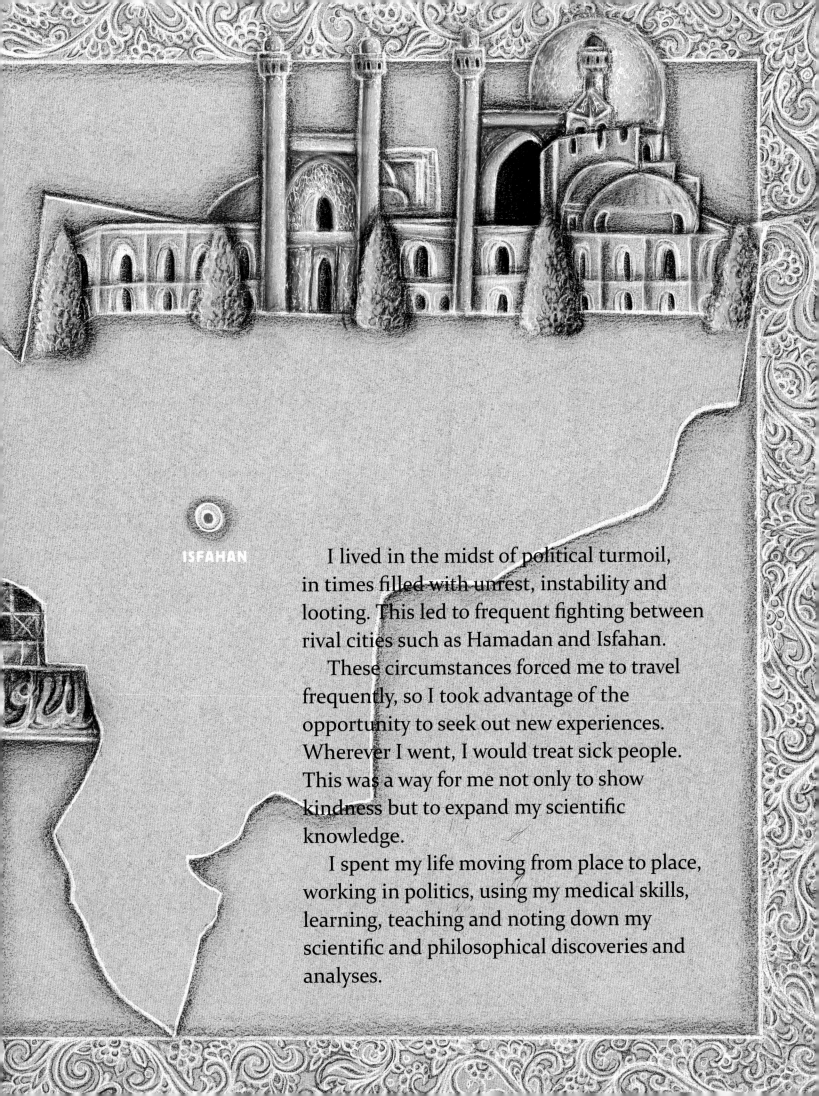

ISFAHAN

I lived in the midst of political turmoil, in times filled with unrest, instability and looting. This led to frequent fighting between rival cities such as Hamadan and Isfahan.

These circumstances forced me to travel frequently, so I took advantage of the opportunity to seek out new experiences. Wherever I went, I would treat sick people. This was a way for me not only to show kindness but to expand my scientific knowledge.

I spent my life moving from place to place, working in politics, using my medical skills, learning, teaching and noting down my scientific and philosophical discoveries and analyses.

One of my major findings was that humans are distinct from animals in the way that they can marvel at things, laugh and cry. The most important features that characterize humans are their ability to speak, use symbols and signs, think abstractly and deduce the unknown from known facts. These abilities are not caused by physical sensations but are due to an independent force, which at the time I called "the self."

I was very interested in education, and I wrote books on this subject in Arabic and in Persian. My fundamental theory was that learning begins from the moment of birth, not at the age of six when a child enters school. Caregivers should pay attention not only to children's mental development, but to their emotional, physical and social development, too.

The first years in a child's life are the most crucial, because in this period the child develops a personality as well as good and bad habits. It is important to give children a nice name at birth so that they develop a positive self-image. I also stressed the benefits of breastfeeding, which maximizes their immunity and protects them from a variety of diseases later on.

I wrote that
it is essential for
a teacher to be aware of
the personal differences among children,
and to guide each child according to their
capabilities and talents. I emphasized
the concept of reward and punishment,
but not on the physical level. The teacher
should redirect a child's behavior kindly,
not harshly or violently.

I believed in the importance of
teaching children right from wrong and
encouraging them to follow religious
teachings. Through all my writings, I
hoped to reach as many people as possible.

Today they say that I was one of the most brilliant thinkers and eloquent writers of my time. Despite all the political turmoil I lived through, I was able to write more than two hundred books on subjects such as architecture, mathematics, philosophy, music, chemistry, education, medicine and meteorology.

In the science of nature, for instance, I discovered that light travels faster than sound. During a storm, we see the lightning before hearing the thunder. I also discovered that sound travels in ripples. We do not see the ripples go through the air, but without them sounds would not reach us.

Many of my books have been preserved to this day, and some of them have been translated into various languages and reprinted several times.

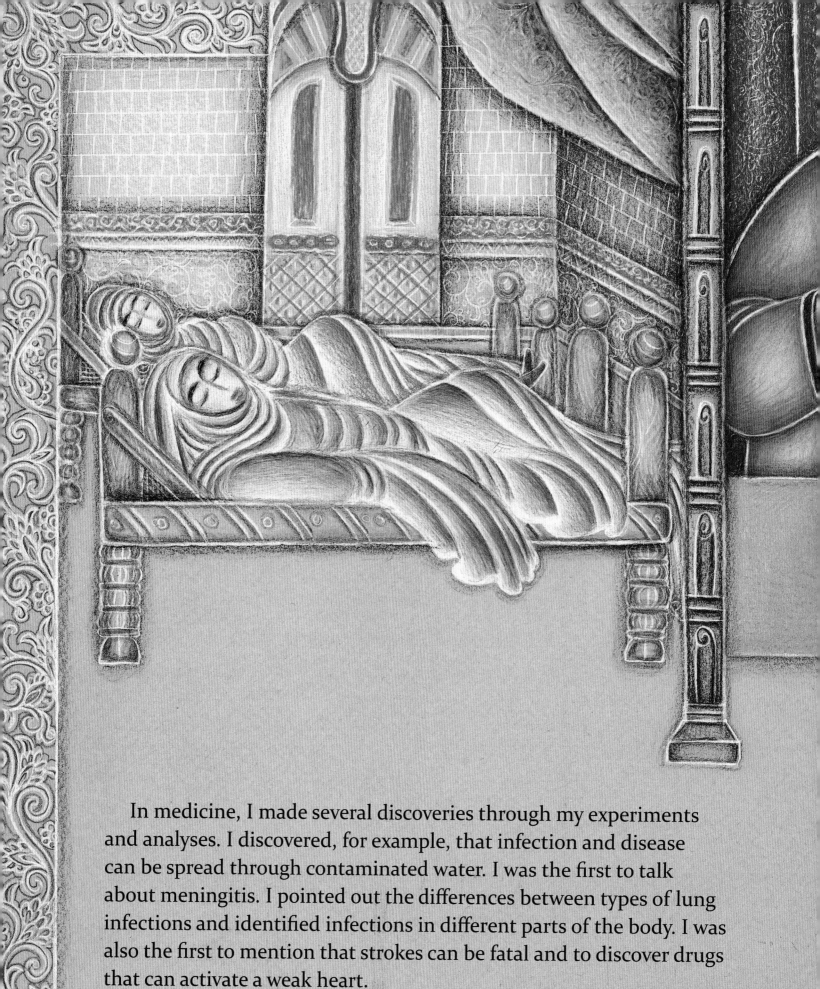

In medicine, I made several discoveries through my experiments and analyses. I discovered, for example, that infection and disease can be spread through contaminated water. I was the first to talk about meningitis. I pointed out the differences between types of lung infections and identified infections in different parts of the body. I was also the first to mention that strokes can be fatal and to discover drugs that can activate a weak heart.

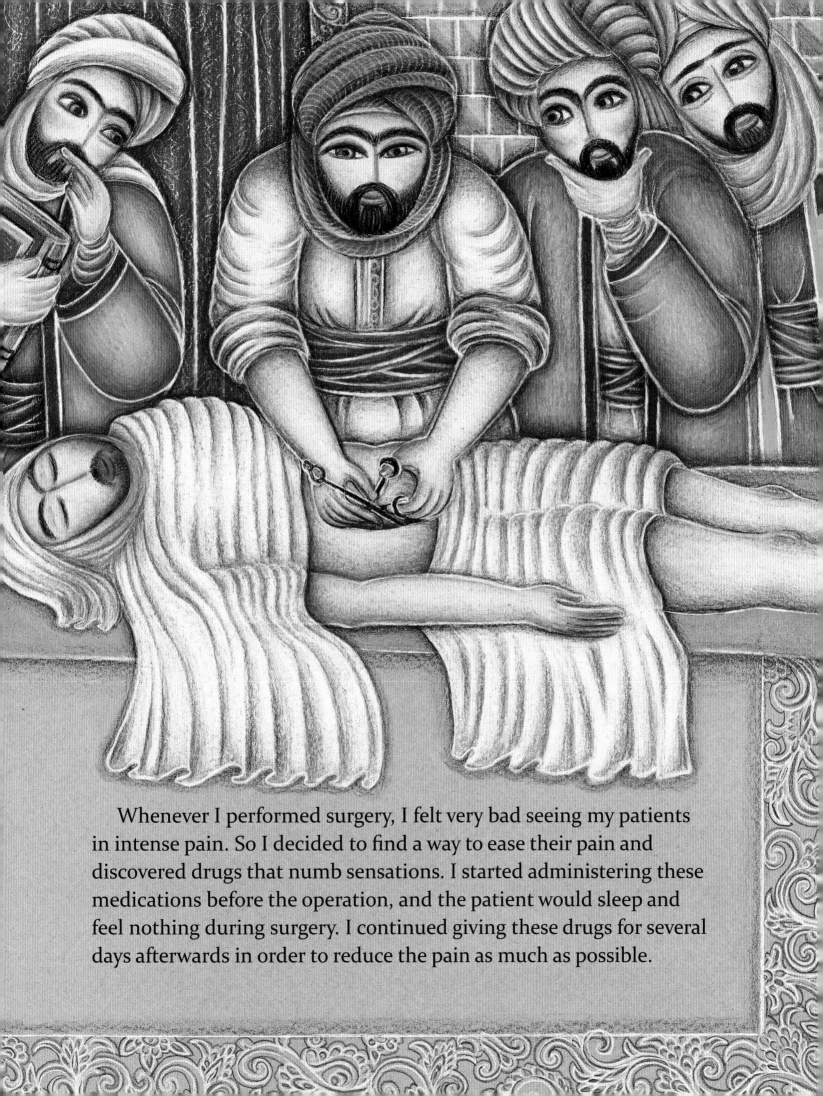

Whenever I performed surgery, I felt very bad seeing my patients in intense pain. So I decided to find a way to ease their pain and discovered drugs that numb sensations. I started administering these medications before the operation, and the patient would sleep and feel nothing during surgery. I continued giving these drugs for several days afterwards in order to reduce the pain as much as possible.

My most famous work is The Canon of Medicine. It is a collection of books in which I explain all matters relating to the human body, including various diseases and how to treat them. I also list the names of medications and surgical instruments.

The Canon of Medicine was translated into several languages and became one of the most important sources for teaching in the universities of the Islamic world and Europe. It was used as a major reference through the 1700s.

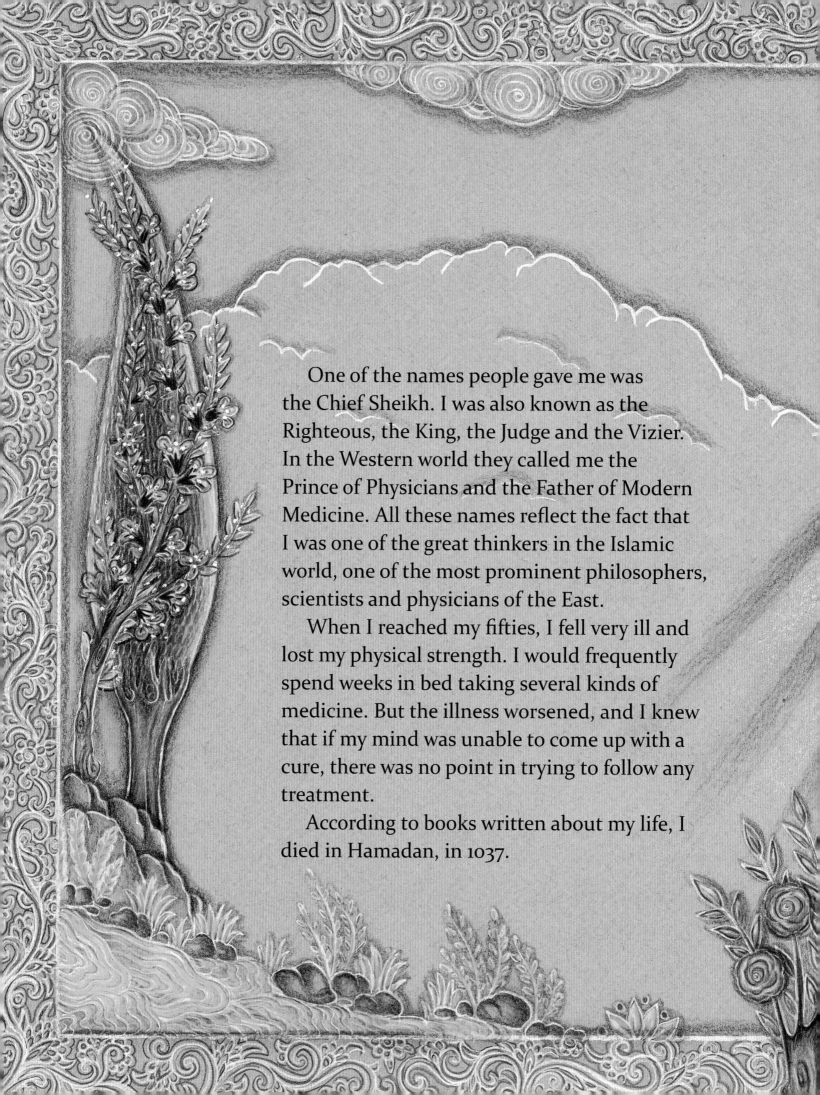

One of the names people gave me was the Chief Sheikh. I was also known as the Righteous, the King, the Judge and the Vizier. In the Western world they called me the Prince of Physicians and the Father of Modern Medicine. All these names reflect the fact that I was one of the great thinkers in the Islamic world, one of the most prominent philosophers, scientists and physicians of the East.

When I reached my fifties, I fell very ill and lost my physical strength. I would frequently spend weeks in bed taking several kinds of medicine. But the illness worsened, and I knew that if my mind was unable to come up with a cure, there was no point in trying to follow any treatment.

According to books written about my life, I died in Hamadan, in 1037.

Author's Note

Ibn Sina was a genius of the Islamic Golden Age (c.622–c.1258) — a time when Arab and Islamic scholars, philosophers, researchers and scientists thrived in various fields of discovery. Our hero was a polymath, distinguished by his historically crucial contributions in the medical field. His famous work, The Canon of Medicine, has made his name live through the centuries.

It is essential, in my opinion, for new generations of children to be introduced to such historical figures, especially since school curriculums in most parts of the world do not include them.

The manuscripts of Ibn Sina that have survived to this day are preserved in various locations. The Süleymaniye Manuscript Library in Istanbul is believed to have manuscript copies of all his surviving works. The Aga Khan Museum in Toronto has the earliest manuscript of The Canon of Medicine, and the Bibliothèque nationale de France in Paris has a complete online version, as well as several other manuscripts.

Fatima Sharafeddine

First published in 2013 in Arabic as *Ibn Sina* by Kalimat
P.O. Box 21969, Sharjah
United Arab Emirates
www.kalimat.ae
Text copyright © 2013 by Fatima Sharafeddine
Illustrations copyright © 2013 by Intelaq Mohammed Ali
First published in English in Canada and the USA in 2015 by
Groundwood Books
Text copyright © 2015 by Fatima Sharafeddine

Groundwood Books / House of Anansi Press
110 Spadina Avenue, Suite 801, Toronto, Ontario M5V 2K4
or c/o Publishers Group West, 1700 Fourth Street
Berkeley, CA 94710

We acknowledge for their financial support of our publishing program the Government of Canada through the Canada Book Fund (CBF).

Library and Archives Canada Cataloguing in Publication
Sharafeddine, Fatima, author
The amazing discoveries of Ibn Sina / written by Fatima Sharafeddine ; illustrated by Intelaq Mohammed Ali.
Previous title: Ibn Sina.
Issued in print and electronic formats.
ISBN 978-1-55498-710-8 (bound).—
ISBN 978-1-55498-711-5 (pdf)
1. Avicenna, 980-1037—Juvenile literature. 2. Islamic philosophy—History—Juvenile literature. 3. Medicine, Persian—History—Juvenile literature. 4. Muslim philosophers—Biography—Juvenile literature. 5. Physicians—Iran—Biography—Juvenile literature. I. Ali, Intelaq Mohammed, illustrator II. Title.
B751.Z7S53 2015   j181'.5   C2014-906796-8
                                      C2014-906797-6

The illustrations were done in color pencil.
Printed and bound in Malaysia

MIX
Paper from responsible sources
FSC® C012700
www.fsc.org